It's Wedding Season
A Prophetic Call to God's Women in Waiting

By
Dr. Cubeon Pitts

© 2019 Cubeon Pitts

All rights reserved. No portion of this book may be reproduced, photocopied, stored, or transmitted in any form – except by prior approval of the author or the publisher, except as permitted by U.S. copyright law.

Printed by
Divine Empowerment Publications
Huntsville, Alabama

Unless otherwise noted, all Scripture quotations are taken from the NEW INTERNATIONAL VERSION of the Bible.
Printed in the United States of America

U.S. Copyright No. Pending: 1-7328262941
ISBN: 978-0-578-45051-3

Table of Contents

Acknowledgments 4
Foreword by Yvette Benton.. 6
Introduction... 8

Chapter 1: Why Do You Want to Be Married?................ **17**
    Kingdom Marriage 20
    Are You Ready for Marriage 24
    Daddy Issues... 32
    Altered Personality.. 33

Chapter 2: Finding Courage to Hope Again..................... **37**
    Your Plan vs. God's Plan 38
    Don't Bend to the Pressure of Time 45
    Your Fulfillment 50

Chapter 3: It's Wedding Season **55**
    Kingdom Couples.. 56
    Soulmates.. 58
    Inner Healing.. 59

Chapter 4: Soul Ties.. **63**
    Illegal Soul Ties... 65
    Secret Lovers 65
    Only Healing Heals Wounds 70
    Severing Illegal Soul Ties 71

Chapter 5: Only Healing Heals Wounds **77**
    Seek Godly Counsel 78
    Preparation Is An Offensive Strategy 81
    Intimacy.. 82

Chapter 6: A Living Sacrifice **87**
    Your Flesh Must Die... 89
    Realistic Expectations 93
    Ready to Say 'I Do' 104

Contact Dr. Cubeon Pitts.. 108

Acknowledgements

I must give honor where honor is due and give thanks to Jesus Christ to whom all of the glory is due. Without God, this would have been impossible. Thank You, Daddy-God, for trusting me with the unique mission of preparing Your daughters for marriage. I'm grateful that You continue to use me in spite of me. To God be the glory for the marvelous things He has done, is doing, and will continue to do through me.

I dedicate this book to my Momma-Dukes, my late mother, Idella "Dee" Pitts. You never wanted me to follow in your footsteps, suffering in a domestically violent relationship. By the grace of God not only do I have a different story but God is also using me to change the marriage trajectory of many others.

I want to thank my mentor, Yvette Benton personally. I came to you for counseling for inner healing so I wouldn't repeat my family's history of having a destructive marriage, but I received so much more. I knew from our first appointment we were divinely connected, and my life would never be the same. Thank you for surviving your past and pouring your wisdom into me. I'm following you step-by-step. Please know if you never do anything else for me, you've done more than enough.

To my family and friends, thank you for sharing your marital experiences with me. I appreciate you taking the time to tell me the good and the bad you've experienced in marriage. I'm grateful to have your support.

Special thanks to my Vessels of Valor sisters for encouraging me through the process of writing this book. I'm excited about doing ministry with you. I have a group of sisters who are holding me accountable for maintaining a standard of holiness on this journey of singleness. I'm incredibly blessed because I know when I transition to being a helpmeet, you'll still be by my side holding me accountable to being a Kingdom wife. Dr. Katrina Foster, thanks for the push and encouragement to finish this project. I appreciate the time you spent reviewing my "baby" and providing me with great insight and a fresh perspective. I couldn't have done this without you.

Foreword

From the moment I began talking to Dr. Cubeon Pitts, I knew something was different. By different, I mean special and unique. We discussed the various views we developed about relationships and how the Holy Spirit completely challenged our "natural" way of thinking. She shared with me that she was not married but desired to be completely ready spiritually to be the best wife and mother possible. I was immediately intrigued and excited. Finally, I had found someone who thought the way I had learned to think. Her insight and desire to get everything "right" with God was inspiring.

I have since come to know her well. She is most definitely a prophetic voice that God uses in a prolific way. She has a keen insight into the heart of God and her wisdom and ability to teach and preach her revelation is far beyond her years. I'm honored to have her as an intercessor and more honored to cover her spiritually.

Given the work she has put into her own healing and deliverance, I know her testimony will heal and encourage many. The message of healing before helping is one that has often been overlooked and misunderstood. This book will bring much-needed clarity, not only to the unmarried but to the married person that may not have healed emotionally before marriage. A lack of healing and deliverance from past hurt, trauma and experiences results in relationship bondage. I encourage all who read this book to use it as a spiritual guide to relationship freedom.

Yvette Benton

Impart Ministries International/Gerald and Yvette Ministries (GYM)
BSW Social Work
M.A Counseling, Marriage and Family Therapy
Ed.S Educational Leadership

Introduction

I never wanted to be the poster child for singleness and have to wait a long time for marriage, yet here I am. I'd be happy being married with children, praying for all the single souls in my position. I'd be happy to support the person that had a long wait and ended up achieving fame because God used his or her story of singleness to touch people all over the world. That's really sweet, but I don't want it. All I've ever wanted was to be married with children, yet here I am lying in bed with tears rolling down my face, writing the book I never wanted to write out of obedience to God. This morning I should be at work, but I couldn't find the strength to pull myself out of bed just yet.

While laying here, the Holy Spirit spoke to me and said, "They're waiting." Immediately, I knew He was talking about the people that would read the book I didn't want to write. I wish I could tell you my response was "Yes, God" with enthusiasm. However, the truth is I told God I didn't care, then rolled over and cried myself back to sleep. I couldn't understand why God was asking me to do this. God, haven't I done enough? I don't want to travel down memory lane to painful parts of my past. I don't want to relive the pain of the things I'd gone through to help people who will read my book. All I wanted was for my husband to come so we could live happily ever after. Now my happily ever after was contingent upon my obedience.

When I woke up from my crying induced nap, I had a decision to make. Absolutely nothing in me wanted to write the book you're holding in your hands. I laid in bed thinking about what I was going to do next. Could I ignore my first love, Jesus? Could I ignore the nagging at my heart? Could I live with knowing I disobeyed God willfully? No. At the end of the day, I love God, and I must show Him that through my actions. I'm not religious. I have a personal relationship with the Father, and because of that, I cannot ignore Him. I told God I would serve Him, and that means putting His desires before mine. Many of us have asked these same questions. Can you recall a time when God spoke to you in the midnight hour to do something you really didn't want to do? What did you do?

As I said previously, I can't willfully disobey God, so I'm beginning this book on my phone, lying in bed, on this windy Thursday morning. By the time you read this, I believe I'll be married. Okay, I just hope I'll be married. I think that would give a sweet ending to this book. However, my timing is not God's timing, so you and I both have to wait to find out how my story ends.

It's very easy to whisper sweet promises to God in the middle of worship when we're surrounded by His presence. It's very easy to do what God is asking us to do when He's asking us to do something we want to do. It's very easy to trust God when you haven't been holding on a long time, and you still have your strength. However, it is a difficult thing to trust God when you've been waiting a long time, been disappointed several times, you're exhausted, and God is asking you to do things you don't understand or desire to do.

Yet it's in this place that the people who genuinely love Jesus are separated from the religious who are merely following traditional religious customs. After all, Jesus tells us if we love Him we'll keep His commandments (John 14:15). In John 14:23, Jesus also says those who love Him will do what He says (NLT). In these scriptures, the Lord is telling us that our love is an action of choice. Love is a verb. It's not enough to say we love Jesus, but our efforts and lives bare no fruit of that love. I love Jesus. I really do! I don't love Him for His *presents* but for His *presence*. It's my love for God that fuels my radical obedience to push through the tears, push pass my self-centered feelings, and write this book as the Lord has instructed me to do.

One of the reasons I didn't want to write this book when the Lord began to impress upon my heart to do so is because I typically don't care to read books on singleness. The things I've read that were geared towards singles have an underlying message, saying singles should be thrilled to be single. I refuse to do that.

I realized that the Lord wasn't asking me to be like anyone else. I believe there needs to be a balanced perspective, and that's what I bring in this book. I'm not going to validate your depression about being single. I'm not going to validate your hopelessness. I'm not going to agree with you on how hard it is to find a good man. That's not my role in writing this book. My objective is simply to position you to be better prepared for your marriage journey.

I want you to know all of the feelings you have about your singleness are real. While everything that you feel is real, your feelings, however, may not be true. For example, the hopelessness that many singles feel is real, but it isn't true. There is always hope. The point I'm making is that your feelings are real, but sometimes they lie to you. I won't tell you how you should feel. That's a personal pet peeve of mine. No one should tell you how you should feel, but you need to be aware that your feelings aren't your best friend and sometimes they lie about your circumstances. I teach a balanced perspective on singleness. I want you to be encouraged, and I want you to have a realistic understanding and expectation for marriage. Otherwise, you can end up with another problem after saying I do.

Right now, I don't know everything that's going to flow from my heart on the following pages. Just know I'm writing to singles like me from a place of much hurt and loss, but also from a place of hope. I pray that one day I'll be able to say that all the tears I cried were worth it because of the testimonies that will come from people reading about my story, my heart, my pain, my preparation, and prayerfully a love story with a happy ending. I desire that you will learn from my experiences and apply the spiritual concepts I share with you in this book.

Obviously, I'm not a wife, but I am in a season of divine preparation to be a Kingdom wife. God has led me to understand that the season of singleness is purposeful, and this is what we are to be pursuing while we are single. In obedience to the Lord, I'm sharing what I've learned with other singles. By the time you finish reading this book, you will be divinely strengthened, encouraged, and positioned to be a Kingdom wife. God will make you a bride. Get ready. It's wedding season!

Declaration

I decree and declare that as you continue reading this book, your mind will be renewed according to Romans 12:2.

Do not conform to the pattern of this world, but be transformed by the renewing of your mind. Then you will be able to test and approve what God's will is—his good, pleasing and perfect will.

ROMANS 12:2

May the words on these pages provide Godly wisdom in accordance to Proverbs 2:6-8.

For the Lord gives wisdom;

from his mouth come knowledge and understanding.

He holds success in store for the upright,

he is a shield to those whose walk is blameless,

for he guards the course of the just

and protects the way of his faithful ones.

PROVERBS 2:6-8

The Word of God is a light guiding me (Psalm 119:105) into my Kingdom marriage. I declare it's wedding season!

So the Lord God caused the man to fall into a deep sleep; and while he was sleeping, he took one of the man's ribs and then closed up the place with flesh. Then the Lord God made a woman from the rib he had taken out of the man, and he brought her to the man. The man said, "This is now bone of my bones and flesh of my flesh; she shall be called 'woman,' for she was taken out of man." That is why a man leaves his father and mother and is united to his wife, and they become one flesh.

GENESIS 2:21-24

Chapter 1

WHY DO YOU WANT TO BE MARRIED?

The steps of a good man are ordered by the LORD, And He delights in his way.

PSALMS 37:23 (NKJV)

The success of a marriage is predicated on following biblical principles. You can have what the Word of God says you can have if you do what the Word of God tells you to do. Your steps have been ordered. The first step on your journey to marriage is examining why you want to make this lifelong commitment.

Why do you want to be married? It's important to understand why you want to be married. Marriage is beautiful, but like everything else in life, it requires maintenance. For example, if you're blessed with a brand new, luxury vehicle, you'll have maintenance. That vehicle will require a specific type of gas, oil changes, tire rotations and balance, and a host of other types of maintenance as the vehicle ages and increases in mileage. Marriage shouldn't be entered into lightly. The Apostle Paul tells us he would prefer everyone stay single like him.

> *I say this as a concession, not as a command. But I wish everyone were single, just as I am. Yet each person has a special gift from God, of one kind or another. So I say to those who aren't married and to widows—it's better to stay unmarried, just as I am. But if they can't control themselves, they should go ahead and marry. It's better to marry than to burn with lust.*
> 1 CORINTHIANS 7:6-9 (NLT)

The Holy Spirit asked me why I wanted to be married. I fired off my answers:

- I want to love and be loved.
- I want a family.
- I am tired of being alone.
- I want to have sex within covenant.
- I want someone to do life with.
- I want someone to help pay these bills.
- I want someone to help me through the hard times.

Through my process of marriage preparation that you are about to read, my reasons for wanting to be married changed tremendously. My method of preparing for marriage has been frustrating, to say the least. Unknowingly, I fought God when all He was doing was trying to get me what I asked for – the fairytale relationship I desired. Fairytale relationships do exist but not without sacrifice.

Do you recognize anything about my list of reasons why I wanted to be married? All of my reasons for desiring marriage were about me and something I craved. Going into marriage with this mentality is a setup for disaster. The first problem was that I didn't understand that marriage is not about self, yet all of my reasons for wanting to be married were about myself. I was ignorantly selfish in my thinking about marriage. When two people enter marriage with a mindset of wanting to serve the other person, it can be a fairytale, just not a Disney fairytale. Marriage is servitude. When you marry, you agree to become a living sacrifice.

The wife gives authority over her body to her husband, and the husband gives authority over his body to his wife.

1 CORINTHIANS 7:4

Kingdom Marriage

Everything God has created has a purpose, including the family unit. The family is important to God. For your family to function and thrive the way God intended, there must be Kingdom order. The Word of God gives us the hierarchal structure of the family.

The head of every man is Christ, and the head of the woman is man, and the head of Christ is God.

1 CORINTHIANS 11:3

Men are the leaders in their homes. Wives are to submit to their husbands as the Word of God tells us. This word submission almost feels like a profane word to most women. I was included in that number. I remember having a frank conversation with God many years ago, telling Him I'm okay with everything in His Word except the part about wives submitting to their husbands. I had a hard time accepting this truth because of my background. Growing up in a domestically violent home, with a father who abused his authority, made me loathe the idea of submitting to any man. After all, women are equal to men. Wives walk beside their husbands not behind them. All of this is true. Yet and still, the husband is the head, and wives are to submit to their husband's leadership. God holds men responsible for the state of the family. Not respecting your husband's position as the head of the home puts him in an awkward position. If he's ultimately responsible, then he should have the decision-making authority.

Of course, this does not mean your future husband shouldn't heed your advice. He can't be a successful leader in your home without your input. However, you need to respect him as a leader and use wisdom in the way that you offer your advice. There will be times that your husband will make a bad decision, and you see the terrible outcome coming a mile away. Instead of lashing out, telling him he's stupid or saying or doing anything else disrespectful, you need to take the issue to the Lord in prayer. My best advice to future helpmeets concerning this is to pop a bag of popcorn and watch the movie *War Room*. If you want to learn how to cover your family, learn from the Miss Clara, the elderly lady in this movie, who teaches women how to "war" in prayer.

In Proverbs 21:1 (NLT), the Bible says, "The king's heart is like a stream of water directed by the Lord; he guides it wherever he pleases." Take your issues with your husband to the Lord, and He will turn his heart. You have a responsibility and a right to pray about your husband, however, you are not the executor. Only God can execute change in your husband. Your responsibility and strategy is to "war" in prayer. The Lord's intended structure and functionality of the family unit is outlined in Ephesians chapter five.

Wives, submit yourselves to your own husbands as you do to the Lord. For the husband is the head of the wife as Christ is the head of the church, his body, of which he is the Savior. Now as the church submits to Christ, so also wives should submit to their husbands in everything. Husbands, love your wives, just as Christ loved the church and gave himself up for her to make her holy, cleansing[a] her by the washing with water through the word, and to present her to himself as a radiant church, without stain or wrinkle or any other blemish, but holy and blameless. In this same way, husbands ought to love their wives as their own bodies. He who loves his wife loves himself. After all, no one ever hated their own body, but they feed and care for their body, just as Christ does the church—for we are members of his body. "For this reason, a man will leave his father and mother and be united to his wife, and the two will become one flesh."[b] This is a profound mystery—but I am talking about Christ and the church. However, each one of you also must love his wife as he loves himself, and the wife must respect her husband.

EPHESIANS 5:22-33

Are You Ready for Marriage?

There is work for you and me to do during the singleness stage, and that is the basic premise of this book. To be blessed by the message in this book, you have to be real with yourself. Everyone has something they need to work on improving. There are three tell-tale signs you are not ready for marriage.

1. **You would rather die than stay single the rest of your life.**

While you're in the season of singleness, you need to come to terms with some of the spiritual strongholds keeping you from entering into what God has for you. You have made marriage an idol. If marriage is an idol, you're not ready for it.

The first commandment instructs us not to have any other gods before Him (Exodus 20:3). While it may be innocent when you say I can't live as a single person, what you are inevitably saying is you need a man more than you need God. This feeling comes out of innocence, but it is wrong. If you were to marry someone while you have this mindset, your marriage is destined for trouble because you would be looking to fill a God-sized hole with a man. No spouse can fill a God-sized hole. Your spouse could never meet your expectations, and your unmet expectations would cause your marriage to fail- even a divinely arranged marriage. As long as you are in this place, you are not ready for marriage. Everything that you are seeking can actually be found with God, not man. Your spouse cannot make you happy. If you are unhappy as a single person, you will be miserable as a married person. Happiness is internal; it originates from within. As long as you feel as though external forces control your happiness, you will be unhappy regardless of your relationship status. Your happiness is your responsibility.

I've known people who thought marriage would bring them happiness, only to learn that it did not. They had unrealistic expectations. They had to learn within the marriage that the intimacy they wanted was with God.

...The joy of the Lord is your strength.
NEHEMIAH 8:10

I was one of those people who felt like I couldn't live without being married. I don't know how many times I told

God in prayer that if I do not get married, He can just take me. I genuinely preferred to be in heaven with Him and my mother over living life as a single person. The loneliness I felt was so real and evasive, sometimes I even felt physical pain. I have since come to understand something I heard Dr. Cindy Trimm, a prophetic minister with a global ministry, say, "Loneliness is the absence of purpose, not a person." The more I delved into my purpose, doing the things God created me to do, the more my loneliness void filled up with purpose. More on that later.

2. **You have not healed from past traumas of physical abuse, emotional abuse, molestation, rape, growing up in a broken home, or divorce.**

Everything you have been through has marked you in some shape, form, or fashion. You may have even put these events and experiences in the back of your mind and moved on with your life. Unless you have purposely sought healing, there is residue on your soul from these experiences.

My friend, Dr. Kenya Rawls, who is a pastor and phenomenal counselor, once said something profound that's always stuck with me, "You're not responsible for your hurt, but you are responsible for your healing." It's true. Our healing is our responsibility. It would be foolish to expect the people that hurt you to heal you. Even if they wanted to, they couldn't. Inner healing is a job for Abba Father.

Spending time in the presence of God, Abba Father, brings healing. Reading your Bible on a daily basis and entering the presence of God is crucial. However, sometimes inner healing comes easier with external help. I urge you to read books that relate to what you're dealing with and see a Christian counselor. There are some things you can't get through alone. Counseling is a safe place to share what's happened to you. Counselors can provide an objective perspective on your situation, teach you coping mechanisms, and even help you figure out what's eating you inside. Everyone has blind spots, things in their life that they can't see clearly, and counselors have an unbiased perspective of your blind spots. This type of objective viewpoint is crucial in the healing process because we tend to look at situations and people through our past experiences and not for what they really are.

Healing also includes forgiving any and everyone who has wronged you. There's a saying that unforgiveness is like drinking poison and expecting the other person to die. It's true. You need to do yourself a favor and forgive those who've wronged you, violated you, betrayed you, stolen from you, and hurt you in any way whether on purpose or not. Unforgiveness robs you of joy and happiness in your present life and guarantees the future won't have any happiness either. Sometimes people choose not to forgive because they feel like forgiveness is saying what was done to them was okay. That's not true. Forgiveness frees you from the bondage of your past. When you forgive, you choose to no longer allow the people that hurt you to hold you hostage. Unforgiveness controls your emotions, thoughts, and actions. Unforgiveness will impact your relationships, making it hard for you to trust innocent people because of what your violators did. Unforgiveness robs you. Don't let another day go by in bondage. Free yourself.

Forgiveness isn't an option for the believer. The Word of God tells us we must forgive others so that God can forgive us. The scriptures have a lot to say about forgiveness.

Be kind and compassionate to one another, forgiving each other, just as in Christ God forgave you.

EPHESIANS 4:32

And when you stand praying, if you hold anything against anyone, forgive them, so that your Father in heaven may forgive you your sins."

MARK 11:25

But if you do not forgive others their sins, your Father will not forgive your sins.

MATTHEW 6:15

Give, and it will be given to you. A good measure, pressed down, shaken together and running over, will be poured into your lap. For with the measure you use, it will be measured to you."

LUKE 6:38

Bear with each other and forgive one another if any of you has a grievance against someone. Forgive as the Lord forgave you.

COLOSSIANS 3:13

3. You have no real-life examples of the biblical representation of a husband and wife.

According to the United States Census Bureau's website, since 1960, the percentage of children growing up in a single-parent household has nearly tripled. People raised in single-family households did not have the advantage of seeing marriage modeled before them on a daily basis. If you're from a single-parent household and desire to be married, you're attempting to accomplish something you've never seen.

Many of the people who grew up in a two-parent household, did not have a representation of a husband and wife modeled before them that was representative of the Kingdom of God. If you have not taken the time to find out for yourself what the Kingdom model of marriage looks like, you are essentially entering into marriage blind. Do you know a couple who is a Kingdom representation of a husband and wife? If you do not know of any healthy couples who are happily married, you can still get the information you need. The internet has numerous Christian resources on marriage. Here is a list of the Christian resources that I've used:

1. Jimmy Evans of Marriage Today – Marriage ministry

    https://marriagetoday.com

2. Book: *The 5 Love Languages* by Gary Chapman

    https://www.5lovelanguages.com

3. Gerald and Yvette Ministries – Marriage ministry

    https://GeraldandYvette.com

4. Book: *The Power of a Praying Wife* by Stormie Omartian

    https://www.stormieomartian.com

You are blessed to be loved by the Lord, to be chastened and purified by Him in this season, and then you get to be a wife in a God-ordained Kingdom marriage. Some people don't get the opportunity to heal from past traumas and experiences before entering marriage. Count it a blessing and a joy. Many people have had to walk through the process of inner healing while in a marriage covenant with someone else who needed healing, and that person may or may not have been seeking healing. You have an opportunity to work it out beforehand. God values you enough to pull you out of this cycle saying, "I've ordained you for marriage, and I want you to enter it whole, lacking nothing." God wants to piece your broken heart back together with His anointing.

Daddy Issues

I've heard people say marriage shows you yourself. That marriage will show you who you are at your core. This idea always made me nervous. I knew I had daddy issues from growing up in a domestically violent home, and many of these issues would not surface until I was in a romantic relationship. I was nervous about finding out what was inside of me. It seems so silly looking back on it now. At the time, I didn't know I could discover what was rotting at the core of my soul beforehand.

I have dealt with my daddy issues. I urge you to deal with your issues, whatever they are. My inner healing process was comprised of consistent time in the presence of God and counseling. Your inner healing process should consist of natural and supernatural means. Prayer is an absolute necessity, and you cannot be healed without it. However, sometimes you need to talk to someone. Depending on the person and the trauma experienced, a professional counselor or therapist may be necessary to achieve healing. Don't despise receiving formal counseling. Get the help you need. Issues not dealt with will rear their ugly head in your marriage.

Altered Personality

Our experiences shape the way we see the world and the people within it. Unbeknownst to you, your past experiences have altered your personality. Some of how you respond and handle altercations and stressful situations are shaped by the things you have experienced. In these instances, your character may have been altered. Your experiences may have developed some of your mannerisms. Often, we make excuses for our behavior by making comments like, "Well, this is just who I am." But, in reality, it is not who God created you to be. Do not condone behaviors that are not Godly and that do not line up with the Word of God.

Let me give you an example. Your introverted nature may very well be a result of child molestation. As a child, you may have withdrawn as a coping mechanism, learning it was safer to stay in your shell. The abuse is in your past but you never "came back out." Another person who has been in a domestically violent relationship may have learned to be quiet out of fear of being scorned. Even though that person is far removed from that awful relationship, they may have never regained the courage to speak up for themselves. They may consider themselves as quiet. However, the truth is they need to find their voice again. I urge you to ask God in prayer what parts of your personality have been altered by the trauma you have experienced.

Prayer

Father, show me the areas of my personality that have been altered due to the past trauma I have experienced. Lord, heal my soul and my mind from the pain. Restore my personality and character to the way You created me to be. Please help me to accept the reality that there are parts of me that are not the real me. Give me the strength and courage to change. Give me the boldness to be who You created me to be. I cancel the assignment of the spirit of memory recall that forces me to relive the trauma in my past and the pain associated with it. In Jesus' name, I pray. Amen.

My prayer for you

Father, for the women who read these pages, I pray that the eyes of their understanding of marriage and its purpose would be enlightened. May their desire to be self-seeking in covenant marriage decrease as their desire to love like You increases. Use this book to speak to the innermost parts of their hearts and souls as they proceed. In Jesus' name, Amen.

Chapter 2

FINDING COURAGE TO HOPE AGAIN

"For I know the plans I have for you," declares the Lord,
*"plans to prosper you and not to harm you, plans to give you
hope and a future."*

JEREMIAH 29:11

A person in the process of believing God for something must take the clock off the situation. Instead of thinking in terms of days, months, and years, take it one hour at a time. When that's too much, take it one moment at a time. While waiting for God's perfect timing, remove the clock so you don't have an internal pressure persuading you to move outside of God's will and timing. You don't know how long it will take but wait on God's timing. God's will and desires for your life are far beyond marriage. God is doing great things right *now*. He wants to use you *now*. He wants you to walk in purpose now. He wants you to have joy *now*. Find what you're supposed to be focused on *now*. Your purpose doesn't begin when you say I do. It begins *now*. Identify your purpose and operate in it *now*.

Your Plan Versus God's Plan

My life was planned out. I planned to finish college, get married, have children a couple of years later, and do it all by the age of twenty-six. Again, that was *my* plan. As of now, I am a few weeks away from turning thirty-six. I'm not married, and I have no children.

For as long as I can remember, I have always wanted a summer wedding. My birthday is in November. I always felt like my parents shortchanged me on my birthday and Christmas gifts. I remember them saying I could not have something for Christmas because they bought something for my birthday. Other times, I would ask for something for my birthday, and they would tell me if I got it, I would not be able to have something else for Christmas. My sibling, whose birthday is in the spring, never had that problem. I vowed as a little girl to marry in the summer, so I could always get a nice anniversary present from my husband and enjoy beautiful weather on vacation when celebrating my anniversary. I had it all planned out.

I cannot remember a time that I did not desire to be married. I dreamed of my wedding day as I played with my Barbie dolls as a little girl. When my family took the eight-hour drive to my grandmother's home, I was excited about the hours of uninterrupted daydreaming the trip would provide. I'd have time to daydream about having a husband and family of my own. Year after year after year, I hoped and waited with expectation. Years passed. Eventually, a decade passed. Unmet expectations turned into anger. Anger turned into discouragement. Discouragement turned into numbness. I never told anyone, but I often wondered if I could ever truly give and receive love if and when my husband came because of the dullness that surrounded my heart from the numbness. I dared not share that with anyone.

During the years that I have waited in expectation of marriage, I rested my faith on a fairytale wedding. I remember the day I told God I wanted a fairytale wedding. Days later, I walked into a Benny Hinn healing conference with a friend. Out of the blue, I heard, "You're getting married!" My friend and I both turned around, looking for the person talking and the person getting married. She repeated it, and I looked around but did not see anyone. She pointed to me and told me she was talking to me. I considered whether she was a prophet or simply crazy until she tells me I'm having a fairytale wedding. How could she know that? I merely whispered that to God days ago. That encounter took place years ago.

As my single years continued to roll by, my desire for the perfect summer, fairytale wedding began to wane. I accepted the harsh reality that my late mother would not be a part of my big day. I accepted the fact that I had not experienced motherhood while my friend's children were growing older each year. It was during this dry season that I accepted the call of God on my life to preach and began to settle down in my singleness. I was no longer angry about my unmarried state.

Despite my desire for the perfect fairytale wedding, I continued my tradition of selecting a day that I wanted to be married at the beginning of each year. I do not recall where I got the idea, but I've done it for years. I wanted my wedding date to be a particular date that had meaning to me. This particular year, the wedding date I selected was August 18th, 08/18. It was the perfect sequence of numbers and the last opportunity for this type of sequence of numbers during the summer months. Plus, this day was on a Saturday. It was the perfect day for a wedding. Of course, I wondered if God would allow me to get married on this date. After all, He never instructed me to pick a date each year. This was a plan I constructed on my own.

As it got closer and closer to August, I began to get nervous thinking about the level of miracle it would take for me to meet a man, date him, get engaged, and be prepared to marry with such short notice. Once August arrived, I was hurt but not surprised. A few weeks prior, Holy Spirit began asking me to let the date I had selected go. When August 18th came, I had to fight to keep my soul from propelling into depression. I spent that day in much prayer, which kept me sane and out of depression. After the date passed, I decided I'd had enough of this game. Never again would I pre-select a wedding date. I came to terms with my situation and was at peace. I no longer cared about having a particular wedding date.

As I previously mentioned, I had long let go of the desire for the perfect, fairytale wedding day. I no longer cared about having a big, beautiful wedding. The wait made me realize that the only thing I needed was my husband. Everything else was extra. If no one else showed up, I would be okay. If I got married in a courthouse, it would be okay. I waited so long I lost the desire for the frills and thrills. I was at peace. My lack of desire for the frills and thrills was partly a coping mechanism to protect myself from being hurt in the event it never happened.

That is when Holy Spirit came in like a flood, destroying the peace I had established in my mind. He was asking me to plan a wedding, look for wedding rings, try on wedding dresses, and pick a wedding date for the next year. I was angry and confused. Why would God deny me what I wanted to the point of me losing interest just to demand me to plan again? It felt like God was toying with my emotions. If the purpose of the wait was to make me realize what was truly important, I accomplished that mission. I genuinely no longer wanted these things. Once again, I was angry with God for forcing me to do something I did not want to do. To add insult to injury, God was asking me to plan a wedding while I didn't have a boyfriend.

Out of obedience to God, I did everything He asked me to do. I tried on wedding dresses and researched wedding venues. I went store to store trying on engagement rings. It was also scary because my mind was telling me not to hope because it will hurt to be disappointed again. I fought those thoughts, and to my surprise, it was fun doing everything the Lord asked me to do. Now, I'm in the waiting room, and I know God is looking at my attitude while I wait. I'm finally waiting well with a good attitude.

How are you waiting? Are you waiting in expectation? Are you angry with God that you're still single and so many of your friends have already gotten married? Are you offended that people who aren't as "good" as you married before you? Do you have a promiscuous friend who married before you? Are you trying to understand why you're not married when you've been abstinent? There is no clear explanation why some people marry earlier than others. Everyone's story is different.

It's hard to watch others receive their miracle when you're still waiting on yours. It's hard even when you're genuinely happy for other people. Everyone, at some point in life, must go through the test of watching others receive the miracle they need. Instead of being discouraged, be encouraged. God is no respecter of persons (Acts 10:34). You have to know God is faithful to His Word in the scriptures. What He does for others, He will do for you. Your miracle, however, may be wrapped differently and arriving at a later date, but it will arrive.

Here's an extra tip: The waiting doesn't stop when you get a ring. You're partnering with God for that man to come into the fullness of who God created him to be. You'll do that throughout your marriage. Right now, you're waiting for that man to show up. Once you're married, you're still waiting for that man to show up. You see, God has given each man giftings and anointings. As a wife, or as I refer to them, a helpmeet, you partner with God to pull those giftings out of that man and help him operate in the anointings God has given him. Helpmeets do just that—help their husbands. It's a fantastic partnership.

The role of a helpmeet is similar to Holy Spirit. The Word tells us in John 14:26 that Holy Spirit is a comforter; helpmeets provide comfort to their husbands. Holy Spirit is an intercessor; helpmeets intercede on behalf of their husbands. Holy Spirit is a strengthener; helpmeets strengthen their husbands. I really like the way the Amplified version of the scripture describes our comforter, Holy Spirit.

But the [a]Helper (Comforter, Advocate, Intercessor—Counselor, Strengthener, Standby), the Holy Spirit, whom the Father will send in My name [in My place, to represent Me and act on My behalf], He will teach you all things. And He will help you remember everything that I have told you.

JOHN 14:26 (AMP)

Don't Bend to the Pressure of Time

Don't allow your frustrations to move you out of God's will for your life and cause you to miss what God has for you. Do you have an internal clock that seems to beat faster and faster with each passing year? Many singles have an internal stopwatch that's counting down how much time they have left as an eligible bachelorette before no one will ever want them. Some singles have a stopwatch counting down how much time they have left to be able to conceive a child. Some singles have a stopwatch counting down how much longer they'll be able to wait in abstinence before willfully falling into the sin of fornication. Please take a moment to think about what internal clocks you have telling you that you're running out of time. Don't bend to the pressure of time.

The pressure of time leads to desperation. Desperation to meet a schedule that you came up with leads to bad decisions. Desperation for a spouse, family, and children can pressure you to step outside of God's will, which will, in turn, cause you to miss what God has for you.

This wisdom key applies to all areas of your life. You never want to be so desperate for something that you're willing to do anything to obtain it, including going outside of the will of God. Anything you go outside of the will of God to get you'll have to stay outside of the will of God to keep. Again, don't bend to the pressure of time.

If God has spoken to you and told you who your husband is, you have to allow God to show him. It's not your job to tell your future husband you're his wife. He should be receiving his directive from God. It's not your role to speak to him concerning the matter. That's between him and God to execute. If he chooses not to follow God's directive, he will be outside of God's will. You won't. God will not hold you responsible for his decision. Rest your faith here... at the end of the story, you will be happily married. Remember, the Lord is not slow in keeping his promises (2 Peter 3:9).

And without faith it is impossible to please God, because anyone who comes to him must believe that he exists and that he rewards those who earnestly seek him.

HEBREWS 11:6

He who finds a wife finds a good thing,

And obtains favor from the Lord.

PROVERBS 18:22 (NKJV)

Bending to the pressure of time will cause you to settle for anything outside of God's perfect will for your life. Don't allow the pressure of time to cause you to miss out on the blessing of a good and right man for you. The deafening silence in your home from the absence of a man can tempt you into settling for being with a man who you know you shouldn't be with. The immense pressure from your family, friends, co-workers, society, and church to "hurry up and settle down" is insurmountable, but do not bend to the pressure of time. Don't settle for a piece of a man. Don't settle and give your body away because you don't want to wait for a man who will agree to abstain from sexual relations until marriage.

Believe that God will never ask you to wait for something that wouldn't be worth the wait. Don't bend to the pressure of those telling you that your standards are too high. If God has spoken anything to you, regardless of whether its marriage related or not, stand. Stand on the Word of God.

Stand on the prophetic word. Sometimes you will have to stand by yourself.

Sometimes God tests us. He will allow you to stand for something that only you know and can see. Sometimes He gives you a vision for something that He's not given anyone else in your life. He hasn't shown your pastor what He's shown you. He hasn't shown your parents. He hasn't shown your mentor. He hasn't shown your best friend, but He has shown you. Sometimes you are the only person with the vision, and there is incredible pressure to conform to what others are saying. When times are tough, ask God to give you something to hold onto to help your faith stand the test of time. Whatever you do, do not give up. It will be worth the wait.

I share this with extreme caution. Those who are spiritually immature can take this message and use it as an excuse to make a decision that their flesh is driving under the guise of "God said it." For the record, I do believe someone in spiritual authority over you should bless your union. If you genuinely believe the Lord has shown you who your spouse is and your spiritual leadership does not yet see that vision, wait. Do not enter the covenant of marriage without confirmation from your spiritual leadership. It may be the right person at the wrong time.

Your Fulfillment

When you're married, your fulfillment should be in God, not your spouse. The fulfillment you need is a God-sized hole, not a man-sized hole. When you rest your expectations of fulfillment on God, you free your spouse from unnecessary and unrealistic burdens. You alone are responsible for your happiness. Please take a moment and think about it.

It's important to cancel and release the fantasies you created in your mind. If you marry with the fantasies you have in mind, you will inevitably try to change your future spouse into the man you envisioned. It's important to remember your fantasy is just that, a fantasy. It's not real. Do not attempt to shape your partner into something you have envisioned. Your future spouse is an individual. They will want to be accepted the way they are, the same as you desire.

Singles who desire marriage sometimes have an expectation that their spouse will fulfill them, but singles should really be looking to God for fulfillment. As a single, you should feel complete and whole. That does not mean you shouldn't desire marriage. That desire is natural and healthy. The problem occurs when someone feels like they can't be happy unless they're married. Once upon a time, I was like that. The profound loneliness I felt grew into an unbearable pain, and no aspirin could ease my agony. I was so lonely there were days I literally hurt. Have you ever experienced loneliness that echoed so deeply within your soul you literally felt pain?

Earlier I shared that loneliness isn't the absence of a person but the absence of purpose. I believe this to be true because of what I experienced. As I began doing the things I loved and operating in the giftings and callings God put in me, the loneliness began to fade. One day I realized it had been months since I last ached with the pain of loneliness.

Now that isn't to say you won't and shouldn't desire companionship. Having company is nice. I still desire to have someone to spend time with. As a matter of fact, I got a dog several years ago so there would be someone happy to see me when I came home. I totally get it. It's incredible how loud silence can scream when you come home to an empty house after work. My puppy Jellie-Bean was a far cry from the testosterone and muscles I desired to have hugging me, but she was good company and great to cuddle. Again, a simple desire for companionship isn't evil. I'm talking about loneliness. You're lonely when you cannot be happy without someone else. I want to talk to you about loneliness and your desire for a spouse.

Many singles misinterpret the internal longing for purpose as the longing for a spouse. If you're unfulfilled today and get married tomorrow, you'll simply be an unfulfilled married person. Marriage doesn't complete you. Too many singles think getting married is going to fulfill them only to cross over to the other side and find out it doesn't. I've talked to many married people who told me marriage wasn't what they thought it would be. Marriage didn't bring the overwhelming joy they thought it would. Do you know why? Marriage doesn't bring you joy; you bring joy to the marriage!

Many singles have not investigated and researched what it means to be married, so they don't know what married people are saying about how marriage isn't what they thought it would be. Ask around. Talk to your married friends, church members, and coworkers. Ask them what they wish they had known before saying I do. Based on my conversations, I ascertain that they were looking for their spouse to fulfill a need that couldn't be met by a human being. Interestingly, many of them didn't report that their marriages were bad, just that it wasn't what they thought it would be. They had unmet expectations. Had their expectations been appropriately aligned and realistic, they would not have so many unmet expectations in marriage.

More often than not, married people have shared with me that marriage is a lot of work—more work than they realized. They'd heard people say marriage was a lot of work, but they underestimated the extent of that work. Your marriage will be off to a great start if you have a realistic understanding of the work involved to have and maintain a healthy marriage. Marriage is a lot of work, but the reward is great. It's my prayer that after reading this book, you'll enter marriage with realistic expectations, increasing your chances of not only staying married but also remaining happily married.

Prayer

Lord, help my unbelief. I confess the times I've doubted You and Your word, and I ask for Your forgiveness. Help me to rest in Your unfailing love for me and Your promise in Jeremiah 29:11. I smash the internal clock pressuring me and telling me I'm running out of time and that it's too late for me to start a family. Your timing is perfect. Everything is working together for my good. I lay aside my desires for Your perfect will for my life.

Show me if I have an unhealthy desire for marriage. Help me to lay aside false expectations that are setting me up for disappointment. Father, I give You this loneliness in exchange for Your peace and joy. Fill me. I desire nothing and no one above You. Thank You for interrupting my daydreaming with a reality check. I know that You love me and will give me what's best for me in Your timing. Please forgive me for believing otherwise.

In Jesus' name I pray, Amen.

Chapter 3

It's Wedding Season

He who finds a wife finds what is good and receives favor

from the Lord.

PROVERBS 18:22

It's wedding season!

As a prophetic voice, the Lord often speaks to me a word to share with His people. One day while I was out driving, I heard the Lord say, "It's wedding season!" It was as if I had downloaded a large file from the heavens. Holy Spirit began to show me several things about this season that He referred to as "wedding season."

In this season, marriages are being divinely arranged. The dating time is going to be super short. The engagement time is going to be super short. It's a season of prophetic acceleration. The importance of understanding this and taking advantage of your remaining time as a single is imperative because you will not have the time to prepare for marriage when your future spouse arrives on the scene. Thus, heaven has mandated me to spread a message of urgency to prepare for marriage.

And the two shall become one flesh; so then they are no longer two, but one flesh. Therefore what God has joined together, let not man separate.

MARK 10:8-10 (NKJV)

Kingdom Couples

The men and women who God is bringing together in this season have a Kingdom purpose, which is something to do together that benefits the Kingdom of God. God wants you married more than you desire to be married. He knows what He created you for. Not only does the Lord God desire for you to be married, but He also desires for you to be successful at it. The couples that He's bringing together in this season will be power couples. They will have wealth and influence to accomplish their Kingdom missions. Their purpose will be far-reaching, beyond the four walls of the church. Some of these power couples will be entrepreneurs operating a business together. Their purpose extends beyond raising children and going to church on Sunday morning.

This is wonderful news! However, as the Holy Spirit shared this excellent news with me, He also revealed that His people are not ready. While the Lord our God is arranging for new marriages to come together, the enemy is lying and waiting to attack these marriages. If we as singles do not take the time to prepare for marriage in our singleness adequately, our marriages will not last. If we don't prepare, we could end up divorced. There are people divorced today that God put together. Marrying the person you were created to be with does not make your marriage divorce-proof. Marriage is two imperfect people coming together. Regardless of God bringing people together, there is still work to be done right now. Marriage is serious, and a marriage arranged by God still requires a lot of work. Some people may think the problems in their marriage mean they made a mistake by not marrying their soulmate. This is not true! If Jesus knocks on your front door and stands there saying this is your wife, this is your husband, the marriage will still require work. Please get out of your mind that the marriage will be "easy." Marriage takes work to work. Two imperfect people coming together to accomplish anything will always require work.

Soulmates

As a romantic, I believe in soulmates, someone created just for you. If God cares enough about us to count the number of hairs on our heads, surely He cares about the person we choose to spend the rest of our lives with. That's not to say I believe there is only one person for us. I simply believe God brings men and women together.

It's absolutely crucial to differentiate between soulmates and soul attachments (commonly referred to as soul ties). The soul is comprised of the mind, will, and emotions. Often people become soulishly attached to someone they shouldn't be connected to and become convinced this person is their soulmate because of how they feel about them. The truth of the matter is their souls have become illegally entangled, thus creating a soul tie. I'll discuss soul ties in more depth in the next chapter.

Indeed, the very hairs of your head are all numbered. Don't be afraid; you are worth more than many sparrows.
LUKE 12:7

Inner Healing

It's wedding season, and this season consists of a lot more than buying a wedding dress and saying I do. This season includes a process of preparation that involves inner healing and tearing down wrong mindsets and systems of negative thinking that come against the knowledge and person of God. This process involves getting rid of idols. If you're dealing with trauma, God wants you healed from that trauma so you can be whole and help your spouse on their journey. This is especially important because men are less likely to ask for help or read a book like you're doing now. By the time your husband shows up, you'll need to be emotionally available to help him through his deliverance. It's wedding season, but you have to get ready.

Many people see wedding season as a time for premarital counseling, fittings, buying the perfect dress, selecting the bridal party, food tastings, cake selection, rehearsal dinners, and finding the perfect wedding hashtag. All of these are wonderful, but they're preparing for the wedding event. This event only lasts a day. As I've walked out my own personal preparation for marriage, I've discovered that the wedding season is more about preparation for the marriage, not so much the wedding. If you have the heart to be married, rest assured God is going to bring His plans and purposes to fruition in your life, and that includes being *happily* married.

It's a privilege to come to this awareness of the need for inner healing and preparation. There are a lot of married people who didn't have the opportunity presented to them. What is this opportunity? It is the opportunity to minimize and eliminate marital issues. When you're healed, you create fewer problems in a marriage. When you're healed, you respond better to negativity. When you're healed, you're in a better position to help someone else heal. When you're healed, your vision is clear, allowing you to see your spouse and situations as they truly are. When you're not healed, you see people and situations through the pain of past experiences, making it possible to have a good thing and be completely incapable of seeing it and appreciating it.

Be grateful that you have the opportunity to get it right first. If you're a divorcee, count it a blessing to have the opportunity to further capitalize on your past experiences by going into your next marriage whole. In this season of preparation, God has called you to go through this process so you can be a helpmeet and have a marriage that represents God's perfect love for the church. Your season of singleness can turn into a blessing.

For all singles, there is a blessing in the waiting. There's correction and uncommon favor by being able to be alone in the presence of God. It's wonderful to be able to be called away into the presence of the Lord like the scripture tells us in Song of Solomon 2:10. Yes, you can be alone with God in marriage, but it's different because the dynamics have changed.

Prayer

Lord, prepare me to be a Kingdom wife, a helpmeet suitable for my future husband. I want to be prepared for the marriage, not just the wedding. Show me areas of my personality that can be a hindrance in my marriage. Show me anything in me that can be an issue in my marriage. Use me as a vessel to bring healing and deliverance to my future husband. I choose as an act of my will to make myself a vessel You can use. I give You free rein to do whatever is necessary to prepare me. In Jesus' name I pray, Amen.

Chapter 4

SOUL TIES

Trust in the LORD with all your heart and lean not on your own understanding; in all your ways submit to him, and he will make your paths straight.

PROVERBS 3:5-6

Human beings are three-part beings. Every person is comprised of a body, soul, and spirit. When we die, and our body returns to dirt, and our spirits go to where we spend eternity, heaven, or hell. Our soul is comprised of our mind, will, and emotions. Soul ties are comprised of our mind, will, and emotions being entangled with someone else's mind, will, and emotions legally or illegally. An example of a legal soul tie is the bond shared between a husband and wife. Husbands and wives are to operate as one. However, singles often develop illegal soul ties during the dating process. Having your mind, will, and emotions entangled with someone you're not married to will create distractions, havoc, and prevents you from hearing the voice of God clearly. The presence of illegal soul ties is detrimental when you're trying to establish a legal soul tie through the covenant of marriage. This is why healing from past relationships is critical.

Soul ties are developed by having sexual relations and by forming intimate connections. It's possible to have a soul tie with someone you've never had sexual relations with. It's even possible to have soul ties to someone you have no connection with because of the imagination. Sometimes we, as women, allow our imaginations to run wild about a man who we have no relationship with in real life, and a one-sided soul tie is born. You know you have a soul tie when you can't leave someone alone, when you cannot walk away quickly, or when he controls your thoughts and actions whether or not he's present.

Illegal Soul Ties

I had a soul tie with my mother. We were best friends. My soul tie to my mother became illegal once she passed away. The evidence of that illegal soul tie was revealed in my behavior. Several years after her passing, I was still incapable of sifting through her belongings without having a meltdown. I couldn't throw away any of her items until my soul tie with her was broken. Soul ties aren't limited to romantic relationships; they exist in various types of relationships.

Soul ties are broken by prayer. If you believe you have a soul tie with someone who has passed away, it needs to be broken. If you have a soul tie with an ex-lover, it needs to be broken. If you have a one-sided soul tie with someone you've never met or had a relationship with, it needs to be broken. There's a prayer at the end of this chapter to help you break illegal soul ties.

Secret Lovers

I have experienced walking through the severance of multiple soul ties. However, there was one soul tie that caught me by surprise. I was lying in bed one day, and Holy Spirit began speaking to me about a man I had not been in contact with in years. I was perfectly fine going the rest of my life never seeing him or hearing from him again. We never had sex, but I have to be honest and admit, we did partake in other sexual acts God was not pleased with.

To my surprise, Holy Spirit began showing me this man and I were soulishly attached. I remember very distinctly Holy Spirit telling me that if my husband came that day, he couldn't have my whole heart because this man had pieces of it. Likewise, if his wife came that day, she couldn't have his whole heart because I had pieces of it. I was shocked! At first, I did not believe it, but all of my old feelings for this man came back to the surface- feelings I had not felt in years. I loved this man...secretly. You see, not only did we never have sex, we were never in a committed relationship.

We were *friends*— *friends* who sometimes blurred the line of our supposedly platonic relationship. We were *friends* who would talk and text all day and stay on the phone for hours at night. We were *friends* who fooled around. We were *friends* who prayed together. We were *friends* who spent Christmas holidays together. We were *friends* who met up out of town for vacations. We were *friends* who went on a "couples" vacation with other couples. Of course, I was just filling in since he didn't have a girlfriend. We were *friends* who gave each other advice on all things including relationships. We were *friends* in between his relationships. This on and off again *friendship* went on for ten long years. I never had a boyfriend during this time, but he did date off and on. During the times he was in a relationship, our friendship was strictly platonic and only consisted of talking on the phone.

My *friend* had no idea I secretly loved him. My *friend* had no idea how much I hurt seeing him with someone else. My *friend* had no idea I secretly hoped to one day build a future with him. I was in love with my *friend* for a decade and never dared to tell him out of fear that he did not feel the same about me. I was afraid of being rejected.

I had never laughed and cried so much with one person. I had never argued so much with one person. I had never prayed so much about one person. I had never been so concerned about the opinion of one person. I had never been so hurt. I had never felt so unappreciated. I had never felt so used. Through this, I never realized I was the one to blame.

It was my own insecurities that kept me in a ten-year cycle of happiness, sorrow, anger, and hurt. It was my own insecurity that allowed this to happen. It was my own insecurity and fear that kept me from being honest with my *friend*. It was my own insecurity that made me hold onto something that was dead out of fear that there might not be something better for me. It was my own disobedience that kept me in this toxic mess when God sent someone to me on more than one occasion to tell me this man was not the one He had for me.

I was in love with my assignment. I was in love with a man I was supposed to be praying for. Instead of praying for him, I tried to keep him for myself. My actions proved that I did not trust God to bring the right man because I was afraid to let this one go. Unbeknownst to me, even during the years we did not speak, I kept part of my heart reserved just for him. Have you ever proclaimed that a certain someone would always have a special place in your heart? You can move on and still carry a torch for someone else.

You can get married and still reserve a special place in your heart for someone. This is not the way God would have it for you and me.

My *friend* reached out to me after a few years of no communication. During the years we had not spoken, we had both matured. For the first time, I felt comfortable telling him how I really felt about him. To my surprise, he felt the same. We wasted ten years because we were afraid of rejection. Looking back, it all seemed so clear. We gave each other signs that we cared about each other, but our insecurities blinded us. I asked my *friend* to join me in fasting and prayer to seek God's will for our relationship. He agreed. The secret love we once shared did not mean we had a sufficient foundation to continue our *friendship*.

When Holy Spirit began talking to me about this man, I thought I was over him because I had been okay with not speaking to him ever again. The ugly cry I had in the middle of the grocery store as God revealed the true state of my heart proved to me otherwise. I hurried home so I could cry in private. This cry was a release. This cry was a release of everything I had held on to for ten years. Time does not heal all wounds; it just makes you believe you are healed because your wound is hidden. Time does not heal any wound.

Only Healing Heals Wounds

All of the old feelings started to resurface. The reality of what I had done to myself hit me. This hurt was my own fault. I was disobedient. The Lord sent someone to me at least twice to warn me that this man was not my husband, but I forged on with him having a residence in my soul. I was supposed to be praying for this man of God as his sister in Christ, but instead, I was rolling in the sheets with him. I was praying and hoping God would change His mind because my emotions had gotten entangled. I was in too deep. My emotions were a tangled web of confusion. On one hand, I hoped this man would be my husband because of the love and care I had for him. By the same token, I hoped he would not be my husband because our relationship was unstable and brought so much pain and confusion.

Severing Illegal Soul Ties

In my heart of hearts, I knew God was urging me to release this man from my heart completely. I knew God was saying, "Let him go. I have someone else for him." I was afraid to let this man go without knowing what the future held for me. This situation caused me to be honest with myself and admit that I did not trust God to bring me a husband. For ten years I had been able to go back to this man. Now God was asking me to trust him and shut the door to my heart and soul completely.

The Lord showed me what would happen if I married this man. Holy Spirit showed me that this man could give me his all, and I would still be unhappy, feeling unsatisfied because this man was not designed for me. I will explain it this way. I do not need what is in this man, so even though he could be giving me his all, I would feel unsatisfied, and he would feel unappreciated. Then the Lord showed me I needed a lot of love, more love than this man had to give.

When we marry people not designed for us, we end up unfulfilled. Divorce is the reality for people who are giving their all and are still left unfulfilled themselves. This man was not built to undergird and support the calling on my life. Likewise, I was not created to be his rib and help him. I did not possess the attributes this man needed in a wife. Each man has different needs. I could give him all I have, yet it would be difficult for him to genuinely appreciate what I'm giving him while his real needs go underserved. By giving him all I have, I would feel taken for granted. It's an ugly cycle I hope you never get in.

The Lord told me very clearly that He had someone else for me. He asked me to let go of the man I held on to for a decade and trust that He would bring the right man into my life at the right time. The Lord was asking me to let go of the piece of a man I had and embrace nothing. At least that's what it felt like. In actuality, I had God's promise, but that felt like nothing because there wasn't a person there who I could touch. I didn't have much, but at least I had something. God was asking me to let go of what little I had and trust Him. I laid across my bed sobbing for hours.

In my fragile mind, none of the things the Lord spoke to me would become a reality until I shared them with my *friend*. Part of me wanted to hold what God showed me in my heart and never say anything to him. After all, once I shared this, I knew with all certainty he and I could never be. All future possibilities of us being together would be gone. To be honest, I did not want to let him go completely not knowing what my future held. Therefore, I decided I would not be the one to initiate this conversation, hoping my *friend* forgot, and this would never become a reality. He did not forget.

One day he called and asked me what, if anything, the Lord had shown me about our relationship. Against every feeling I had, I told him the truth. I shared with him how the Lord showed me we had a soul tie and held pieces of each other's heart. I shared with him how if his wife came she couldn't have his whole heart because I had pieces of it and vice versa. I shared how Holy Spirit showed me if we married we would not be genuinely happy because we were not meant to be together.

When I finished sharing what the Lord showed me, I felt my heart slowly ripping apart with each second of deafening silence that passed. I sensed we both knew this was it, and things would never be the same between us. The last time we were together truly was the last time. There would be no more of his passionate kisses that I had grown to love. There would be no more long embraces. There would be no more visits. There would be no more holidays together. There would be no more hope that he would ever be my man.

It felt like God drove a monster truck over the fantasy dreamland that I had created, smashing and leveling everything I had built. Even though all I had was a fantasy, it seemed so real. To me, it was more real than God's promise to give me a relationship that would fulfill me. That is why this cry was a release of everything I had held onto for ten years.

I urge you not to waste the amount of time I wasted. I voluntarily put myself through unnecessary heartache. Seek God first about your relationships. When God shows you something about a person, do not ignore what He shows you. Doing so will be to your own detriment. Also, when people show you who they are, believe them. Sometimes we give them the benefit of the doubt leading to our own detriment.

Take the time that you need to heal from past relationships and trauma. Healing brings clarity of mind. Healing restores your self-worth and confidence. Healing is a detractor of bad relationships. Healing brings self-acceptance which in turn cripples the spirit of rejection.

Pray and ask the Lord to reveal all of your illegal soul ties and to sever them.

Prayer

Father, reveal to me hidden areas of my soul that need to be healed. Heal every broken part of my heart. I sever every illegal soul tie by the power of the blood of Jesus Christ. I choose, as an act of my will, to cancel every illegal soul tie I have with people in my past, whether living or deceased. Restore unto me the pieces of my heart that are being held ransom by people from my past. Remove everything in my soul deposited by the men I've been with. Give me the strength to end toxic, unfruitful relationships and walk away without looking back. Give me a dream of my future to restore my hope. In Jesus' name I pray, Amen.

Chapter 5

ONLY HEALING HEALS WOUNDS

Wisdom is the principal thing; therefore get wisdom: and with all thy getting get understanding.

PROVERBS 4:7 (NKJV)

Marriage is a lifelong commitment, but there is no requirement for long-term preparation before entering into this lifelong covenant. Some states require couples to have pre-marital counseling, which is excellent. However, you shouldn't stop with pre-marital counseling. A few weeks of pre-marital counseling is not enough training and teaching for this monumental assignment.

Study marriage. Your preparation is your responsibility. In my study of marriage, I have had several moments where I had to stop and ask myself if I really wanted to be a helpmeet. I was unaware that I had several unrealistic expectations about my future husband. Studying my role as a helpmeet required me to re-evaluate why I wanted to be a wife. I'm grateful to God that I had the opportunity to discover this as a single and not within marriage as so many others have. This afforded me the opportunity to work on myself and develop healthy realistic expectations before marriage. By reading this book, you have the same opportunity now.

In our society, we spend months planning a wedding that takes one day, but almost no time preparing for the marriage itself. There is nothing wrong with having a beautiful wedding. However, I urge you to spend more time preparing for the marriage than you do the wedding. Your wedding will be over after a few hours.

Seek Godly Counsel

Please seek Godly counsel before entering the covenant of marriage. It is my personal opinion that the church, in general, does not do a good job preparing singles for marriage. I have been to numerous singles conferences and meetings. They usually center on the importance of purity, remaining abstinent, and how we shouldn't be lonely. Most marriage conferences are limited to married people. Of course, I understand that the sensitive nature of some topics may require this. However, singles should be able to be a part of the general sessions in marriage conferences. The enemy is waiting to destroy the divine marriages coming together in this season. The church needs to take an offensive stance against the enemy by preparing singles for marriage with information. Singles need the information shared during marriage conferences.

Singles need to learn the real truth about what happens after saying I do. As I have been studying marriage over the last few years, I realized that I was ignorant in regards to Kingdom marriage. Although I desire marriage, I am grateful to have this opportunity to learn about marriage before entering into it. Knowing what I know now, I am sure I would have been destined for divorce due to my own behavior and unrealistic expectations. Good people get divorced. I know of several, and you most likely do too.

When good people enter into the marriage covenant ignorantly, they struggle and often end up divorced.

You don't have to be a divorce statistic. I love something that Pastor Jimmy Evans of Marriage Today says, and I paraphrase, "You have a one hundred percent chance of success in marriage if you do it God's way." We need to learn God's way of doing marriage. I equate walking into marriage unprepared to walking around blindly on a cliff. Walk on a cliff blindly and your chances of falling off greatly increase.

The Lord is grieved by the numerous divorces that are taking place. Many good people love God and desire to be loved. There are many people in marriages today who are unhappy and feel trapped. The Lord is grieved by that as well. Like any good father, the Lord desires for you to be happily married.

I've been mandated to write this book as a means of getting the attention of singles around the globe with the message of "Get Ready! Get ready! Get ready! Your wedding day is coming!" When your wedding day comes, God wants you to enjoy the wedding and the marriage. Get ready and prepare now! If you desire to be married, before you say I do, you need to understand the role of a husband and wife from God's perspective, not the perspective of a Godless society.

Preparation Is an Offensive Strategy

If you desire a spouse, don't wait until you meet someone to make room for them in your life. This does not mean that you put your life on hold. It simply means to include your spouse in your plans. This is a season of acceleration. I strongly urge you: if you want a spouse, prepare now. If you desire to have children, prepare now. As you begin getting your life in order, prioritize getting your body in order.

As a woman who desires to have children, part of my preparation is preparing my body for pregnancy. I have to admit—aside from losing weight, this was not on my mind. However, in prayer, the Holy Spirit gave me this strategy. I began doing my research and discovered that a body that is alkaline, with a PH of 7.5, is more apt to conceive. I started to make lifestyle changes in my diet as an offensive strategy. I do not know what the future holds. However, I know it involves me carrying a child that is flesh of my flesh. There is no need to wait until I'm married and ready to conceive to prepare. The natural and the supernatural work together. This preparation is an offensive strategy because the enemy can use our poor diets and health conditions as a door to inflict us with infertility issues. It is advantageous to prepare your body in advance to give you and your future spouse the best possibility of conceiving without problems.

Intimacy

Do not enter into the covenant of marriage withholding secrets from your spouse. It is vitally important that you share the traumas of your past with your future spouse before you say I do. Previously, I discussed how your past trauma has shaped and molded your personality. If your spouse knows this information about you, it will explain a lot of your behaviors to them and help them to exercise more patience with you because they will understand why you are the way you are. For example, a woman who has a history of being cheated on numerous times may find it difficult to trust. If her future spouse knows this, he will be armed and prepared to extend more grace to her in this area. Knowing infidelity has been a problem in the past will help him understand the importance of checking in and letting her know where he is. Without this information, he could potentially see her as a controlling when the truth of the matter is her heart has been broken by infidelity multiple times. This is not an excuse for her behavior. However, sharing this information makes it easier for him to help her through the healing process.

Sexual trauma can hurt your relationship both in and outside of the bedroom. There are many men and women with low sex drives, who think their sex drive is naturally low. The truth for many of them is that the sexual trauma they experienced has impacted their sex life negatively. In many instances, the individual may no longer be plagued with memories of the incident. Even in these cases, the residual effects of those experiences linger.

Time does not heal all wounds. Regardless of how long ago an experience occurred, if you have not dealt with it, that trauma can hurt your current life and relationship. Healing is vital. If you have never healed from an experience you had one, five, ten, twenty, or thirty years ago, you may need to receive help walking through the healing process. Healing can come in many different ways. Some people are able to go in their prayer closet, get alone with God, and walk through their healing. Others may need to seek help through a Christian counselor. Before you say I do, ask God in prayer if there is anything in your past that you need to be healed from. The answer might surprise you. There are too many resources available for you to struggle silently.

Keep this in mind: you cannot become one with anyone you cannot reveal your whole self to. You cannot have intimacy with someone you cannot be completely open and honest with. Intimacy requires transparency. Intimacy means into-me-see. If you are not yet in a place where you are able to share your traumatic experiences with anyone, you are not ready for marriage. The deep hurtful things that you are unable to share with your future spouse will inevitably affect your marriage. That's unfair to the other person. The inability to discuss your experience is a tell-tale sign you're not healed.

How can you become one with someone you are unable to reveal yourself to? If you feel that you are unable to share your deepest, darkest secrets and vulnerabilities, it will hinder the two of you from becoming one. Secrets are like fig leaves, hiding certain parts of your soul, preventing your spouse from having access to all of you. That will affect your relationship. The majority of people entering into marriage today are not a clean slate with a soul free of wounds. People entering marriage today have past experiences of divorce, numerous failed romantic relationships, traumatized in some manner, or have had multiple sex partners. Your experiences shape the way you see the world and have impacted your personality in some fashion. It is crucial that you take the fig leaves off before entering into the covenant of marriage and reveal not only who you are but also who you were. If you cannot do this, you cannot be intimate because all of these things, these fig leaves, are in between you and your spouse.

The vast majority of people are not virgins when they enter the covenant of marriage. I would venture to say that the majority of these people have also never taken the time to sever the illegal soul ties to former lovers and those with whom they were emotionally connected. The result is having multiple people connected to your soul and your soul being connected to multiple people.

Imagine this. It's your wedding day. As a bride, there is a long line of men from your past behind you. Behind your groom is a long line of women from his past. As you and your husband exchange vows, you are taking on the soul ties the other person has. Unless the illegal soul ties are broken, you and your husband unite to each other's soul ties. Soul ties make it impossible for you and your spouse to come together as one operating in perfect harmony.

Prayer

Lord, I lay aside my preconceived ideas of what it means to be a wife. I renounce society's views about marriage that don't align with Your word. Help me to be a Kingdom helpmeet. Connect me with Kingdom couples who can pour wisdom into me regarding marriage. Divinely connect me with people who will provide me with Godly counsel.

Piece me back together with Your anointing. Heal the broken places of my heart that can potentially cause me to react and hurt my future husband and marriage negatively. When I meet my husband, help me to be courageous enough to be transparent and share my past experiences with him, so that there won't be any hindrances to our intimacy.

In Jesus' name I pray, Amen.

Chapter 6

A LIVING SACRIFICE

Therefore, I urge you, brothers and sisters, in view of God's mercy, to offer your bodies as a living sacrifice, holy and pleasing to God—this is your true and proper worship.
ROMANS 12:1 (NKJV)

When you leave yourself open, you leave yourself open to the possibility of being hurt. Loving people comes with a risk. Covering people comes with a risk. The assignment can't be done effectively if you wall off your heart. The same wall that keeps out pain keeps out love. How can someone feel your love and the love of God in you with a barrier between the two of you? Does it leave you vulnerable? Yes. Is it worth the risk to help someone? Yes. Is it worth the risk to love and be loved? Yes. Because of the risk to yourself, you should only embark on these types of assignments at the direction of Holy Spirit, who guides and protects what you cannot.

There is a misconception among God's people that God wants us comfortable. He is not as concerned about our level of comfort as we think. We say things like God wants me happy. God does not want me to be mistreated. We tend to believe everything that we "suffer" is an assignment from hell. Jesus suffered ridicule, beatings, and injustice. Our enemy, Satan, was behind the behavior of the people who tortured him. However, the assignment was from God. Jesus became a living sacrifice to save the world. He was uncomfortable. In the garden of Gethsemane, He asked God, "Can this cup pass from me?" He meant is there any other way this can be done. He didn't even wait for God to respond. He immediately said, "But not my will, your will God" (Luke 22:42). God wanted Jesus to save our souls from a hell we very much deserved, which required Jesus to suffer things He did not deserve. This is the ultimate expression of agape love.

God tells us in His Word that we are to be living sacrifices like Jesus, partaking in His suffering (Romans 12:1). Therefore, you have to leave yourself open to being used by God again and again. Yes, you could get hurt. However, if you don't take the risk, someone else could be lost or remain bound by strongholds that they rightly deserve to be in due to the decisions they have made. They do not deserve to be saved, but neither do we. We have to remember we need the same grace and forgiveness someone else needs. In all of this, it is important to be wise. Do not volunteer for battles God did not assign to you. There is safety in being in the right battle. Those are the ones designed for you to win. In everything you endure, know that God will not leave you unrewarded.

Your Flesh Must Die

One night before going to sleep, I asked God to speak to me in my dream and He did. That night I dreamed I was with a group of women in a living room. Yvette Benton, a marriage and family counselor who I had been following on Facebook, was ministering. She began to do personal ministry. When she took me by the hands, my legs got weak, and I fell to the floor. As I lay prostrate on the floor, she stood over me repeating, "The flesh must die." As I was waking up from my dream, I heard her and the Spirit of God repeatedly saying, "THE FLESH MUST DIE!"

This was a phrase I had heard before. In my quiet time with the Lord, as He spoke to me about marriage, He had been telling me my flesh must die. My mindset regarding marriage had been unknowingly selfish. The Lord dealt with me and changed my mindset toward marriage.

Have you ever popped a balloon with a sharp object? I felt like a popped balloon when God destroyed my fantasies of a fairytale marriage. I can honestly say I'm grateful for the reality check now. Had I been left to my own imagination, I would have entered marriage with unrealistic expectations that would have led to great grief, disappointment, and potentially divorce. Unrealistic expectations become unmet expectations. Unmet expectations lead to frustration, heartache, and anger. After being in supernatural marriage preparation, I understand why so many couples end up divorced.

I used to want a fairytale wedding. The real fairytale is a happy marriage. That beautiful wedding dress and wedding day would mean nothing if I were to end up miserable in the days to follow. I'm looking for more than a "Kodak" moment. I want happily ever after, and happily ever after takes work. The Lord began to show me happily ever after requires dying to self. It requires surrendering my will. Happily ever after requires surrendering the list of things I want my future husband to do for me. Happily ever after requires a servant's heart. According to dictionary.com, a servant is a person who performs duties for others, especially a person employed in a house on domestic duties or as a personal attendant.

Before you close this book and swear off reading any further, let me explain. I am in no way asserting that women are their husband's servants. I am merely stating that as followers of Christ, we are servants to God. As God's servants, He has asked us, as women, to be a helpmeet suitable to our husbands. Don't shoot the messenger! Let's go to the Word of God and read what the Lord has instructed us to do.

> *Now the Lord God said, "It is not good (beneficial) for the man to be alone; I will make him a helper [one who balances him—a counterpart who is] suitable and complementary for him."*
>
> GENESIS 2:18 (AMP)

The Lord began preparing me for marriage several years ago. My first encounter was about eleven years ago. I had washed laundry, and my clothes were still sitting in the laundry basket. I looked at the basket knowing I needed to put those clothes away, but I turned my head and walked pass the basket. I heard Holy Spirit's voice so clearly say, "If you were married, you wouldn't leave that basket full of clothes there." I was astonished. Is God really talking to me about my laundry? Why would God speak to me about something as trivial as my laundry? I didn't know it at the time, but God cares about all facets of our lives. He cares about everything, yes, even the minute details of laundry.

Realistic Expectations

Many of us who are single are looking and expecting a man to fulfill us. The reality is we should only be looking to God to fulfill us because He is the only one who can. You should feel whole and complete, lacking nothing. That does not say you cannot acknowledge what a spouse can "add" to your life. However, a spouse is only that, an "addition," to your life.

As an individual, you were created for a specific purpose. The Lord knit you in your mother's womb (Psalm 139:13), and He knew you before He created the foundation of this world (Ephesians 1:4). You were designed for a specific purpose in the world. The circumstances surrounding your conception and your purpose for being born are mutually exclusive. It does not matter if you were an unplanned pregnancy or unwanted pregnancy; God scheduled your birth into this world at a very strategic time. You could have been born any time in history. You could have been born before the days of Jesus Christ's birth. You could have been born during the 1700s. You could have been born during the early 1900s, but God saw fit for you to live and thrive during the twenty-first century. Even if no one else wanted you, please know that God did and still does.

Your purpose in life is more than marriage, and marriage is more than two people sharing their lives together. You have a specific purpose, and your marriage will have a specific purpose. Your union should benefit the Kingdom of God in some capacity.

Before the Lord popped my fantasy bubble of what marriage would be like, I used to sit and imagine marriage as this beautiful fairytale. When I thought about marriage, I thought about how I would meet the man of my dreams, sweeping me off of my feet, wining and dining me, and treating me the way that I always longed to be treated. I imagined a glorious wedding day with all of my friends in the bridal suite with me before the big moment. I imagined standing outside of the double doors to the sanctuary. I imagined the doors magically opening, wedding music playing in the background, everyone standing looking at me in awe as I began the slow walk down the aisle. I imagined my husband standing there at the altar, waiting to take my hand, and lifting the veil that covered my face for the big reveal.

When I imagined marriage, I thought about all of the rainy days that I would be able to be in the house cuddled up with my big and strong husband. I imagined cooking dinner for my husband and my future family and laughing and giggling around the dinner table. When I thought about marriage, I thought about how I wouldn't have to cut the grass anymore. I thought about how I wouldn't have to borrow one of my friend's husbands to help me do something in the house because I'm not very handy. When I imagined marriage, I imagined finally having someone to sit across the table with when I go out to dinner. I often go out to eat by myself, but I have to admit I get tired of it sometimes. It would be nice to sit and have someone across the table to have a conversation.

When I imagined marriage, I imagined those sweet times of discovering that I was pregnant and I fantasized about how I would share the news with my husband. I imagined laying in the bed as my husband rubs my belly and talks to our baby that we can't wait to meet. When I imagined marriage, I thought about making love whenever and wherever before we had kids because in my fantasy world, he didn't have children either.

When I imagined marriage, I imagined having a mother-in-law who would treat me just like her daughter. I imagined Thanksgiving and Christmas holidays with my in-laws filled with laughter. When I imagined marriage, I envisioned having a husband who always knew just what to say when I was feeling down. When I imagined marriage, I envisioned all of the money that I was going to save by having someone to split the bills with.

When I imagined marriage, I envisioned a husband who was strong in the Lord and who had a deep relationship with Jesus. He would be a man sure of his convictions. I envisioned a man who shared the same convictions as me when it comes to pre-marital sex. I envisioned a gentleman who would automatically love me like Christ loves the church. I envisioned a husband who would love to cut the grass, take out the trash, and pump my gas for me. I envisioned a husband who was a white-collar man with blue-collar skills. I envisioned a husband who was great with fixing things. I envisioned a husband who knew his way around under the hood of a car. I envisioned a husband who would gladly take care of all of the maintenance of the house, and I would have absolutely nothing to worry about because my knight in shining armor would take care of it. Not only did I envision him as an excellent mechanic and handyman, but I also envisioned him as a financially stable man. I envisioned him being someone who was excellent with balancing his checkbook, paying bills on time, and completely responsible. I envisioned a man who didn't have any hang-ups. I envisioned a man who didn't exist.

I remember so clearly, one day years ago, sitting at my desk at work and out of the blue, the Lord began showing me the reality of marriage. As He showed me these things, I softly wept and wept and wept, trying not to alarm my coworkers. I didn't want anyone to hear me crying, and I certainly didn't want to explain the truth behind my tears. God was showing me the not-so-fun side of marriage, and at that moment, I wasn't sure if I really wanted it. I wasn't sure after counting the costs that I still wanted something I had been aiming toward for what seemed to be my whole life. It was as if God had driven a monster truck through my dreamland, and everything that I had imagined over all of these years was suddenly crushed.

No, I didn't imagine anything that's bad for a woman to desire in marriage. However, fantasies can be unhealthy because you can get lost in a world that doesn't exist and have a hard time reconciling reality with fantasy. My future husband has a past, and because of his past, he may not come into the relationship being able to do some of the things that I fantasized. Therefore, I need to allow him to be himself and give him room and opportunity to grow and become a better man. He may grow into some of the things I desired. Then again, he may never possess some of those attributes. For example, a man may come into a relationship with no handy skills, but he can develop those skills over time. Then again, he may never develop those skills, and that's okay too. When my future husband shows up, he should be free to be himself without being measured up against a fictional man I conjured up in a fantasy. Your future husband needs to be free to do the same.

I built an idol in my mind about what I wanted in a husband, and there was no way that a real person would easily fit what I created with my imagination. I knew and understood no man was perfect, but my fantasy of a husband didn't take that into consideration. All of the things that I envisioned were good things, but when combined, they created an imaginary person. When women imagine a man, they run the risk of meeting a good man but not giving him a chance because he doesn't compare well to the imaginary man. Your imagination is a powerful tool. Use it wisely.

Marriage won't be all laughs and giggles. I thought I previously understood that because I came out of a home with domestic violence. My late mother, who I love dearly, was in an abusive marriage for almost thirty years. As a child, I always said that when I grew up, I would never marry someone like my father and would never have that type of relationship. I never struggled to believe that good men existed. I can only determine this to be due to God because I didn't have that example in my household. I didn't see the fairytale that I imagined and dreamed of in my house. However, children that come out of abusive homes tend to be creative because they were accustomed to finding ways to "escape" their circumstances by using their imagination. Not only did I have a good imagination, but I also read what the Word of God says about how men are supposed to treat their wives.

Again, none of the things that I envisioned in a husband were terrible. In fact, it's good to have standards, but our standards need to leave room for people to be human. I'm so glad that God tore down my fantasy idols by driving a monster truck through my dreamland, crushing all of my preconceived notions and ideas of marriage. You see I went from living in a household with domestic violence, which was one end of the spectrum, to conjuring up in my mind a marriage on the complete opposite end of the spectrum. Both are unrealistic. It's unrealistic to believe and expect to be in a terrible relationship where you can't be happy. Yes, that's unrealistic. Yet, it's also unrealistic to think you're going to be happy *all* of the time.

While I have your attention, I want to give you one more reality check. It's unrealistic to think that both you and your husband will always be in the mood for sex at the same time. That's not realistic. I doubt you ever took that into consideration in your fantasy. It's time to compare and contrast your fantasy notions about marriage with reality.

If I had it my way, I would've been married with children in my twenties. I'm not grateful to have been single for more than a decade. I am, however, very thankful that God did not allow me to walk into marriage with unrealistic expectations. The weeping I did at my desk was nothing compared to the hurt I would've had if I had been faced with this reality within a marriage. The Lord has mandated me to share with other singles the things that He has shown me to help you be prepared for marriage.

The Lord showed me a cross in a vision. It was my wedding day. I was standing at the back of the sanctuary getting ready to take that walk down the aisle. I was dressed in a beautiful wedding gown. Down the aisle on the altar stood a cross. I understand now that the Lord was showing me that when I say I do, I'm saying I do lay my life down. I do choose to put your needs before mine. I do choose to serve you for the rest of my life. I do choose to take care of you. I do choose to be kind to you even when you aren't kind to me. I do choose to treat you with respect even if you aren't treating me with respect. I do choose to give you my body when you need me and not use it as a means of manipulation or control. Saying I do means I'm ready to die to myself. I don't think I will ever get this vision out of my mind.

When you imagine marriage from now on, I want you to imagine it as your cross. The cross represents laying down one's life through your own free will. Jesus chose to lay His life down. No one took it from Him. He sacrificed His life for us. Neither you nor I deserved what Jesus did for us on the cross. Yet, He did it for us anyway. The cross represents a dying to self. The cross has nothing to do with fairness. You leave behind your desire for a fair life when you get on the cross called marriage.

Your husband is expected to uphold the same standards. However, when we all stand before God, we are only accountable for our actions. That's why God showed me a cross as a representation of marriage. Regardless of how your husband is acting, you have to be loving and respectful. You're required to treat your husband like a king even when he's acting like King Kong. You have to be a peacemaker when you would probably prefer to punch him. If you want to be a wife who pleases God, you have to be kind and loving even when there is nothing in you that wants to be nice. You have to resist the urge to be petty. There's no room for petty in a happy marriage. There's no room for petty on the road to a fairytale marriage. Fairytales do come true, but the path to get there must be paved.

If you think you're going to have a fairytale relationship just because you met your soulmate and you're both

Christians, you're wrong. There is a day of reckoning coming, and your cute, little dream world will be crushed. Great marriages do not just happen because two people perfect for each other fell in love. Great marriages do not happen because two Christians fell in love. Great marriages do not just happen because God brought two people together. Great marriages happen because somebody is willing to do the work.

The reason I say great marriages happen because "somebody" is willing to do the work is because the effort and agape love of one can cover both for a time. We usually hear marriage takes two, but both people may not be giving equal effort. In those times the agape love of one can save a marriage. Granted, marriage should consist of both parties contributing one hundred percent. The reality is that this doesn't happen all the time. Are you strong enough to carry the relationship if need be? Life happens. There may come a time within the marriage when your spouse will go through something so devastating that it changes who they are and changes the relationship. In times of grief, turmoil, and pain, can you carry the relationship? Can you operate in agape love? Can you do it not knowing how long you will have to do it? Can you fill his love tank when yours is deprived? Can you be patient with a husband who doesn't understand his role as a Kingdom husband? If you desire to be a wife, you need to be ready and equipped with the understanding that life may happen. We don't live expecting bad things to happen. We need to know that they can. Life happens, and when it does, you need to be prepared.

The most important takeaway from this chapter is this: The Lord expects you to operate in agape love, regardless of your husband's actions. When your husband makes you upset, God expects you to operate in agape love. When your husband isn't treating you the way you feel you deserve to be treated, God expects you to operate in agape love. It isn't fair but remember there's nothing fair about the cross. When you stand before God, you and you alone are responsible for your actions.

Ready to Say 'I Do'

My answers were different the second time the Lord asked me why I wanted to be married. This time my reasons for wanting to be married were:

- ❖ To love a man the way You love me
- ❖ To help God restore a man who has been broken down and loved wrong
- ❖ To help a man live out his full potential
- ❖ To fulfill the Kingdom purpose ordained for my relationship
- ❖ To have a family that represents the Kingdom of God in the earth

You're ready for marriage when you've been healed from the trauma in your past and when you're ready to make your life a living sacrifice. Make sure you understand the ramifications of your decision before entering the covenant of marriage. Get excited! It's wedding season!

Prayer

Father, I present myself as a living sacrifice to be the helpmeet that You've called me to be. I lay aside my preconceived ideas of marriage. I'm ready to aid the Holy Spirit and be a comforter to my future husband. Lord, I give You permission to shape me and mold me as You see fit to become the wife You created me to be.

I repent of idolizing marriage and desiring it above You. I'm sorry God. I desire You above all. Help me have a balanced, healthy desire for marriage. Prepare my heart and mind for what You have next for me. I believe You desire to give me a family because You gave me the desire first. I choose as an act of my will to bind my will to the will of the Father for my life. I cancel and destroy generational curses in my bloodline that seek to prevent my husband and me from coming together in holy matrimony. I choose as an act of my will to sever myself from spirit husbands and all illegal soul ties. I belong to Jesus and Jesus alone.

Lord, prepare me to be a helpmeet. Prepare me to be the helpmeet that my future husband needs. Prepare me to be able to undergird him and support him.

I decree and declare that I am a wife and mother. No obstacles are preventing my husband and me from coming together. The best is yet to come. I shall love and be loved. I declare it's wedding season, and it's my turn for love and marriage! In Jesus' name I pray, Amen.

"No eye has seen,

no ear has heard,

and no human mind has conceived"—

the things God has prepared for those who love him!

1 CORINTHIANS 2:9

CONTACT DR. CUBEON PITTS

Contact Dr. Cubeon on her various social media platforms:

Facebook: @DrCubeon

Instagram: @DrCubeon

Twitter: @DrCubeon

YouTube: @DrCubeon

Website: www.DrCubeon.com

www.ingramcontent.com/pod-product-compliance
Lightning Source LLC
Chambersburg PA
CBHW031635160426